THE EMOTIONAL INTELLIGENCE POCKETBOOK

By Margaret Chapman

Drawings by Phil Hailstone

"Margaret Chapman has packed a great deal of wisdom into this small package. Unusually, she tells us not only what Emotional Intelligence is but also how it can be practically developed. Read this book, put some of its ideas into practice, and that could change your life."
Michael Chaskalson, CEO, Mindfulness Works Ltd.

"Insightful – outlines how to develop the skills that will ensure you can influence outcomes and get more of what you want, while bringing others with you."
Gladeana McMahon, Chair, Association for Wiltshire College

CONTENTS

CONTENTS

ACKNOWLEDGEMENTS

I wrote the first version of this book in 2001. Then, a key influence was the work of Dr. Hendrie Weisinger, who inspired the five-step model. Today, in 2011, I wish to acknowledge his contribution and also the ongoing support of my partner, Robin Clarke, whose seminal work into the relationship between 'EQ' and stress in frontline police officers is even more relevant today than it was in 2000. A decade on and the environment is tough, stress levels are increasing and the World Health Organisation cites depression as a major health problem in the western world; an increasing economic burden. Developing our self and interpersonal awareness, our emotional and social intelligence was critical in 2001; now it is essential. I want to thank all those with whom I have worked and teachers who have inspired me, in particular those who have enabled me to think differently about 'EQ' and to do this mindfully. My journey continues because of them.

Published by:
Management Pocketbooks Ltd
Laurel House, Station Approach, Alresford, Hants SO24 9JH, U.K.
Tel: +44 (0)1962 735573   Fax: +44 (0)1962 733637
Email: sales@pocketbook.co.uk
Website: www.pocketbook.co.uk

© Margaret Chapman 2001, 2011.

First edition published 2001 ISBN: 978 1 870471 95 4
This revised edition published 2011. Reprinted 2012. ISBN: 978 1 906610 42 5

British Library Cataloguing-in-Publication Data – A catalogue record for this book is available from the British Library.

Design, typesetting and graphics by **Efex Ltd**.   Printed in U.K.

1 INTRODUCTION

IMPACT OF ORGANISATIONAL CHANGE

It was Aristotle who spoke about a rare ability *to be angry with the right person, to the right degree, at the right time, for the right purpose and in the right way.*

How prophetic his words. Over the last decade everything we know about organisations has changed. Working life is not predictable or stable. In 2001 downsizing, rightsizing and de-layering were euphemisms that are now organisational realities. Today organisations are looking to empower and engage employees in order to maximise their talent. Where emotional intelligence was once the new yardstick, now it is taken for granted. Leaders have to be emotionally intelligent and be authentic, have presence and to lead mindfully.

WORDS THAT SHAPED TODAY'S LEADERS

> *Without a doubt I know managers who are not emotionally intelligent and they are not very effective ... they are not good people managers ... they are not particularly good at their jobs ... and they are certainly not the excelling managers that I would be looking at as my role models. The people who are emotionally aware, in my experience, are the people who get the most from you ... will help you to develop ... and ultimately put you in a position to help other people.*
> Young high-flier, major private sector organisation

> *For leadership positions emotional intelligence competencies account for up to 85% of what sets outstanding managers apart from the average.*
> Daniel Goleman, *Working with Emotional Intelligence*, 1998

AIMS OF THIS POCKETBOOK

This book is designed to:

- Outline a model of emotional intelligence (now popularly known as EQ) based on five dimensions or 'steps'
- Provide a framework for developing EQ, your own and others'
- Offer an opportunity to assess your own EQ
- Stimulate your thinking on the changing nature of work and the role of EQ in individual and relational wellbeing
- Support the use of EQ as a coaching and/or organisational change management strategy

Who is it for?

- Internal or external coaches who are charged with maximising talent and potential
- Managers and leaders who want a practical, 'how to' resource to develop their EQ
- Learning & Development (HRD) practitioners who want a short guide and some practical tools to support the implementation and development of EQ interventions

WHAT THIS BOOK IS

When this book was first published in 2001 I did not intend it to be a definitive guide, but a practical resource. Today, the contents remain relevant and its popularity international. The reason is that it achieved its original aim, to be a route map, a way of navigating, what was then (and still is) a complex territory.

Today the field has matured and references to emotional intelligence have found their way into the popular media, TV dramas and everyday language. It is indeed a field which *the pioneers carved out and the settlers have moved in*. Despite this, the original intention to create a starting point that is accessible, informative and inspirational, holds true. And I thank the many people who have let me know that this is the case. The new edition has been fully revised and updated and I hope will continue to prove popular into and through the next decade.

Throughout the book, I use the terms EI and EQ interchangeably, given that EQ has now become the shorthand.

WHAT IS EMOTIONAL INTELLIGENCE?

EI & EQ

EQ is the popular shorthand for emotional intelligence and how it is defined depends on what 'guru' you follow. The original theory of emotional intelligence (EI) was developed by two US psychologists, Peter Salovey and John Mayer, who wrote about it in a scientific paper in 1990. They defined EI as a cognitive ability, that is, a learned ability to perceive, understand and express our feelings accurately and to manage our emotions so that they work for us, not against us.

In other words, no matter whose definition you use, EI is about:

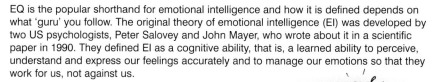

- Knowing how you and others feel and what to do about it

- Knowing what feels good and what feels bad and how to get from bad to good

- Possessing emotional awareness, sensitivity and the skills that will help us to stay positive and maximise our long-term happiness and well-being

Dr Hendrie Weisinger suggests this is simply using our emotions intelligently!

WHY EQ: THEN AND NOW?

While Salovey and Mayer developed the original theory of EI, it was Daniel Goleman who popularised EQ and put this on the organisational map. The original drivers for this were:

- Increasing complexity, globalisation and speed of change
- Rising levels of stress and mental ill health (World Health Organisation)
- Redefining what it means to be a successful manager
- Zeitgeist – a spirit of the times – we talk more about emotions

And now?

- Change is an organisational norm: complex, global and in operation 24/7
- Individuals and organisations need to be resilient
- People manage their own careers; success is internal, psychological
- Findings from neuroscience show that leadership interventions need to integrate mind and body – mindful leaders (Ashridge Journal, Spring, 2011, has more on this)
- The new zeitgeist is about well-being and happiness as a measure of economic success

(11)

INTRODUCTION

WHY BOTHER TO DEVELOP YOUR EQ?

The evidence base for developing emotional intelligence is now overwhelming both in the UK and the US. For example:

- Partners in a multi-national consulting firm were assessed on EI; those high on EI secured $1.2 million more profit*

- Analysis of 300+ top executives showed certain EI competencies (influence, team leadership, organisational awareness, self-confidence) distinguished star performers*

- National insurance company agents weak on EI sold average policies of $54,000; sales agents high on EI achieved $114,000*

- The Centre for Creative Leadership identified that the primary cause of career derailment amongst top executives was the lack of EI*

- Of the sales representatives at a computer company hired on EI, 90% were more likely to finish training*

- A survey of managers in a UK supermarket chain revealed those with high EI experienced less stress, enjoyed better health, performed better and reported a better life/work balance (Slaski, 2001)

*Source for points 1-5 **www.eiconsortium.org**

INTRODUCTION

WHY BOTHER TO DEVELOP YOUR EQ?

- Police officers who are able to identify and manage emotions report lower levels of stress (Clarke, 2000)
- Public Sector Housing Officers report greater levels of cohesion, collaboration and sense of identity following team EI intervention (Chapman, 2004, 2005, 2006*; Clutterbuck, 2007)
- Male and female nurses who possess high EQ experience less stress and lower levels of burnout (Gertis et al. 2005)*
- In nursing, emotionally intelligent leaders influence employee retention, quality of patient care and patient outcomes (Smith et al. 2009)*
- Emotionally intelligent health managers inspire their teams to go beyond the requirements of their jobs (Skinner & Spurgeon, 2005)*

* Contact **mc@eicoaching.co.uk** for copy articles and full references

WHY BOTHER TO DEVELOP YOUR EQ?

If you still need more evidence that EQ is the difference that makes the difference:

- The Harvard School of Public Health predicts that by 2020 depression will be responsible for more lost workdays in the developed world than heart disease
- In the UK the Health & Safety Executive (HSE) Report 2010 noted that stress was the second highest cause of sickness absence – particularly amongst 45-54 year-olds. With an ageing workforce and no compulsory retirement age, this population presents new challenges for people management and development
- When corporations hire MBAs the three most desired competencies are: communication skills, interpersonal skills and initiative
- In the EU 8% of employees have faced bullying
- In 1997 the American Medical Association found that physicians who lack empathy get sued more often
- Assertiveness, empathy, emotional self-awareness and problem-solving skills are more predictive of sales success than background, gender and sales techniques
- Studies of 500 organisations worldwide indicate that people who score highest on EI measures rise to the top of organisations

Source: Fenman, *Using Emotional Intelligence at Work*

THE FIVE STEPS TO
EMOTIONAL INTELLIGENCE

FIVE-STEP MODEL

 INTRAPERSONAL + INTERPERSONAL = EI

| This is the inner-intelligence we use to know, understand and motivate ourselves | This is the outer-intelligence we use to read, sense, understand and manage our relationships with other people |

| 1. Self-awareness
2. Emotion management
3. Self-motivation | 1. Relationship management
2. Emotion coaching |

 The Core Capabilities

THE FIVE STEPS TO EMOTIONAL INTELLIGENCE

MODEL APPROACH

As the model opposite shows, to become emotionally intelligent you have to develop both your intrapersonal and interpersonal intelligence. You do this by focusing on five core capabilities, each one taking you a step closer towards EI.

This chapter looks at each of those capabilities in turn, starting with *self-awareness* which, along with *emotion management* and *self-motivation*, is central to your intrapersonal intelligence – the inner-intelligence we use to know, understand and motivate ourselves.

17

THE FIVE STEPS TO EMOTIONAL INTELLIGENCE

STEP 1: SELF-AWARENESS

There is only one corner of the universe that you can be certain of improving; and that is your own self.
Aldous Huxley

THE FIVE STEPS TO EMOTIONAL INTELLIGENCE

STEP 1: SELF-AWARENESS

Self-awareness is the ability to see ourselves with our own eyes, to be aware of our …

- Goals, immediate and long-term
- Beliefs, about ourselves and others
- Values, those things we hold dear
- Drivers, that affect how we work
- Rules, that we live by, the *shoulds, musts* and *oughts*
- Self-talk, the inner voice that tells us we *can* or *cannot* do something

… and the ways in which these impact on what we do and contribute to our *map of the world*.

Often, some of our inner drives are hidden from our consciousness. Emotional intelligence enables us to access this information by helping us to tune into our responses and identify our *hot buttons* – those core beliefs and values – which, if pressed, evoke the *flight* or *fight* response, trigger an emotion and propel us into action, for good or bad!

THE FIVE STEPS TO EMOTIONAL INTELLIGENCE

STEP 1: SELF-AWARENESS

WHO AM I AS A MANAGER?
INTERNAL AND EXTERNAL DIMENSIONS

Source: adapted from *Why EQ Matters for Consultants and Developers,* Organisations & People, Vol.7, No.1, Dyke, Martin & Woollard, 1999

THE FIVE STEPS TO EMOTIONAL INTELLIGENCE

STEP 1: SELF-AWARENESS

EXAMPLE

Let's look at an example:

You have been asked to carry out a particularly difficult project usually given to more experienced colleagues. You feel valued, trusted and excited. You are also a little anxious *(your self-talk tells you that you are not good enough)*.

Whilst working hard on the project your emotions swing from elation and joy to fear and frustration.

You achieve the task on time and within budget. You feel relieved and proud. You tell your boss and show her your completed work. Your boss gives you no thanks or praise and picks up a minor fault.

You then feel angry and decide that you are never again going to put yourself out. You feel exploited *(self-talk clicks in to reinforce your belief that you weren't good enough)*.

You think about leaving the company *(one of your beliefs is that hard work should be valued and that has been challenged)*. You begin to feel disappointed and upset. You update your résumé and begin to look at the vacancy section.

THE FIVE STEPS TO EMOTIONAL INTELLIGENCE

STEP 1: SELF-AWARENESS

How can you begin to identify the filters (hot buttons) that trigger your emotions, and use this mindfully to achieve positive outcomes?

You can identify your emotional responses by:

- Tuning into your senses in the present moment
- Getting in touch with what these mean, right here, right now
- Becoming mindful of your outcomes (goals)

THE FIVE STEPS TO EMOTIONAL INTELLIGENCE

STEP 1: SELF-AWARENESS
TUNING INTO YOUR SENSES

This means paying attention to what you see and hear and not what you think you see and hear. Your beliefs, values, drivers and rules act as filters, distorting and deleting what otherwise might be important information. A lyric by Simon & Garfunkel in the song 'The Boxer' describes this process perfectly, *We see what we want to see and disregard the rest*.

For example, going back to the scenario with your boss, did she actually pick up on a minor error or was that just your perception? What information did you use to make this appraisal: how she looked or something she did or said that you could have misinterpreted? Alternatively, perhaps some hot button was pushed that triggered what Daniel Goleman calls an *emotional hijacking*, ie: the bypassing of information from our higher *thinking brain* directly to our (older and less developed) *emotional brain* whose evolutionary purpose is survival.

All too often our filters get in the way of information that hit our senses. The higher your level of mind and body awareness, the greater your ability to recognise and distinguish between 'what is' and what is in fact a story you have created based on your filters.

THE FIVE STEPS TO EMOTIONAL INTELLIGENCE

STEP 1: SELF-AWARENESS

TUNING INTO YOUR SENSES

The Map Is Not The Territory
(Alfred Korzybski, *Science & Sanity*, 1933)

People act from their map as opposed to *reality*. Different maps of the same *reality* are of equal value, depending on context. Recognise your map and you open up infinite possibilities of seeing the world in new ways.

Source: figure adapted from The NLP Basic Training Collection Manual Advanced Neuro Dynamics

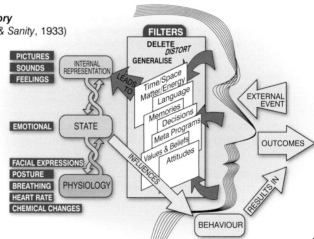

THE FIVE STEPS TO EMOTIONAL INTELLIGENCE

STEP 1: SELF-AWARENESS

 EXERCISE: GAUGING THE MOOD

Now let's try something practical. When you are next in a meeting at work, assess the mood of the group by simply relying on sensory information – what you see and hear.

Seeing:

- Pay attention to how people look at one another whilst they are speaking or listening. Do they look each other straight in the eye (which may indicate confidence)?

- Does the speaker look at everyone or just focus on one individual? (The former could reflect comfort with the group as a whole and a sense of the group being a team.)

- Do listeners stay focused or do their eyes wander? (The former suggests interest in what is being said, the latter indicates lack of interest.)

- Do you see people smile, smirk, frown or glare?

Question: *What impact is this having on me, right here, right now?*

THE FIVE STEPS TO EMOTIONAL INTELLIGENCE

STEP 1: SELF-AWARENESS

 EXERCISE: GAUGING THE MOOD (Cont'd)

Hearing:

- Tune into the sounds in the room, people's voices.

- When a person speaks, is there quiet except for the person's voice or do you hear people moving in their chairs? (The former suggests interest, the latter perhaps boredom.)

- Do people speak stridently (this might reflect anger or frustration) or hesitantly (this might reflect a lack of knowledge of the subject)?

- Do you hear a lot of mumbled conversations while someone is talking? (This could indicate enthusiasm with what the person has to say and eagerness among individuals to comment further. Or, could it denote disapproval, with individuals expressing their disagreement to colleagues?)

Question: *What impact is this having on me, right here, right now?*

THE FIVE STEPS TO EMOTIONAL INTELLIGENCE

STEP 1: SELF-AWARENESS

 EXERCISE: GAUGING THE MOOD (Cont'd)

At the end of the meeting, look at all the information you have collected and see what you can deduce about the mood of the group, based solely on this information.

- Was the team enthusiastic?
- Did they seem pleased that management was willing to try some new idea?
- Did they appear to want to work together as a group to implement the changes?
- Did they all appear to grasp the importance of making the changes?

This exercise shows you how to access mind and body information, to become aware of how you use information to make interpretations. Becoming aware of your own process enables you to use this sensory information, mindfully. Developing this type of self-awareness means that you can make choices about what you see and observe, to achieve your outcomes.

Source: adapted from *Emotional Intelligence at Work*, Hendrie Weisinger

THE FIVE STEPS TO EMOTIONAL INTELLIGENCE

STEP 1: SELF-AWARENESS

GETTING IN TOUCH WITH YOUR FEELINGS

Within psychology there has been a great deal of debate about the exact nature of an emotion. For our purposes, an emotion can be seen to consist of four elements:

1. What we think — our interpretation of events that produces a particular emotional response or thought

2. What we feel — a label that we use to describe a particular state

3. How our bodies react — eg: racing heartbeat, feeling tense

4. How we behave — eg: running away, hitting out or hugging someone

It is generally accepted that an emotion is not simply an automatic physical response to a situation, but our interpretation of bodily changes and information available to us.

THE FIVE STEPS TO EMOTIONAL INTELLIGENCE

STEP 1: SELF-AWARENESS

GETTING IN TOUCH WITH YOUR FEELINGS

Although our feelings are internal, they are often accompanied by outward (often physical) manifestations. By paying attention to these external signals, you can begin to understand what these feelings mean for you, moment by moment. This creates a particular kind of awareness, one that Jon Kabat-Zinn (1994, p.9) describes as purposeful and without judgement.

For example:
- Butterflies in the stomach may mean excitement or fear
- Glowing face may mean embarrassment
- Relaxing into a chair may mean that you are at ease

Certain feelings drive particular behaviours. By becoming mindful in the present moment, of the link between your physical (embodied) response and your interpretation of that feeling you can begin to navigate your emotional responses in any situation. One way of doing this, drawn from cognitive-behavioural coaching and therapy, is to write down changes in your emotional state, by keeping a feeling diary.

THE FIVE STEPS TO EMOTIONAL INTELLIGENCE

STEP 1: SELF-AWARENESS

GETTING IN TOUCH WITH YOUR FEELINGS

Keeping a feeling diary helps you identify your emotional responses. When you notice your mood change, ask yourself: *What is going through my mind right now?* And, as soon as possible, write down your mental image or thought in the *Automatic thought(s)* column.

Date/ Time	Automatic thought(s) What did you think?	Emotion(s) How did you feel?	Response What did you do?	Outcome(s) What were consequences?
	Describe: • Actual event • Stream of thoughts, daydream or recollections leading to the emotions • Any physical sensations	Write down: • Thoughts that preceded the emotion(s)	Specify: • Emotion (eg: sadness, anxiety, happiness)	Detail: • What happened
Example Mon 18th 0930	• Presentation to the Board on new product launch • *I've had no real time to prepare, boss dropped this on me at last minute, we are not ready* • Stomach churning, pressure building at back of neck	• She (boss) should have done this presentation • I'm going to blow it; I know the Finance Director has it in for me • They will see it's not clearly thought through; it will be my fault • I'll look a fool	• Anxiety • Fear	• Just managed to get through • Board not entirely convinced • Asked to re-present in a month

THE FIVE STEPS TO EMOTIONAL INTELLIGENCE

STEP 1: SELF-AWARENESS

GETTING IN TOUCH WITH YOUR FEELINGS

Now, thinking about the example, consider the following questions:

1. What is the evidence that the automatic thought is true? Or not true? *In our hectic business lives today, is there ever enough time or do we do the best that we can within the time available?*
2. Could there be an alternative explanation? *What is the evidence that the boss 'dropped' him in it?*
3. What is the worst that could happen? *Further work needed? (Is this so awful?)*
4. What's the best that could happen? *That the Board don't throw out the ideas altogether.*
5. What should I do about it? *Use it as a learning opportunity.*
6. What is the effect of my believing the automatic thoughts? *Negative thinking evokes an 'emotional hijacking' and undermines performance.*
7. What could be the effect of changing my thinking? *You feel positive, knowing that you have done your best and believe in the work the team has done and what you've got to say.*
8. If you were in this situation, what would you think/feel/do?

THE FIVE STEPS TO EMOTIONAL INTELLIGENCE

STEP 1: SELF-AWARENESS

GETTING IN TOUCH WITH YOUR FEELINGS

Let's take another look at the example:

Date/ Time	Automatic thought(s) What did you think?	Emotion(s) How did you feel?	Response What did you do?	Outcome(s) What were consequences?
Example Mon 18th 0930	• Presentation to the Board on new product launch • *Ideally, boss should do it, but something urgent must have come up* • *Short notice but done my best within time available* • Slight churning in stomach	• Boss given some steer on key players • Finance Director key stakeholder; need to focus on influencing him • Team has worked hard and I really believe in our approach • Feel positive	• Adrenalin pumping, to be expected • Feel anxious but I am going to knock them dead	• Presentation went great • Got the go-ahead to move to launch date (Finance Director particularly convinced by cost-benefit analysis)

THE FIVE STEPS TO EMOTIONAL INTELLIGENCE

STEP 1: SELF-AWARENESS

KNOWING YOUR GOALS

Our goals are what spur us into action. These might be short-term (what we want to accomplish right now/next month) or longer-term (for example, what we would like to have done with our lives).

As with our feelings, our desires or intentions are not always obvious to us. The value of becoming aware of our goals is that we can use this information to help us develop the strategies necessary to get what we really, really want.

For example, suppose you receive a call from an associate who asks you to stand in for him on a project in a week's time. You've recently freed up your diary to write a conference paper, so you could physically do it. However, do you:

- Agree but feel guilty because you have moved other commitments out of your schedule to focus on your writing?

- Say *no* because you have commitments?

- Say *possibly* and leave it vague – you will see what you can do and then get back to him (saying *no*)

THE FIVE STEPS TO EMOTIONAL INTELLIGENCE

STEP 1: SELF-AWARENESS

KNOWING YOUR GOALS

If you decide that:

1. You want to impress your associate with your ability to help out (despite obvious costs to yourself) you will say *yes*
2. You recognise the importance of producing work that is going to contribute to increasing your profile – for long-term success – you will say *no*
3. You want to demonstrate your concern, but really want to say *no*, maybe you will think how both your needs and his can be satisfied

What are the implications?

1. In the first case your underlying motives might be the need to achieve approval
2. In the second, you have a clear sense of direction and what your goals are, and you are prepared to assert your needs to achieve these
3. In the third, you are engaging in avoidance behaviour

What would **you** do?

THE FIVE STEPS TO EMOTIONAL INTELLIGENCE

STEP 1: SELF-AWARENESS

TIPS FOR IDENTIFYING YOUR GOALS

Here are some tips for identifying your goals:

Believe your behaviour
When we are enthusiastic about something, it is because we *want* to do it. If you are
delaying getting started or avoiding a task, ask yourself if this is something you really want
to be doing. Listen to the answer and observe your behaviour. This might reveal your true
intentions. For example, agreeing to stand in for your associate might give the impression
that you are dependable and supportive, but at what costs to your own needs? (How long
before you get back to him to say *no*?)

Trust your feelings, ie your embodied, felt sense
When you feel happy, satisfied or content in a certain situation, it is likely that you are in
alignment with your inner- and outer-self, ie: you are doing what you *want* to be doing
(referred to as being congruent). However, if you have agreed to undertake something and
you feel resentment, it could well be that your original intention is in conflict with some
underlying goal. For example, in the scenario with your associate, you may have agreed to
help him out, but begin to feel angry at his demands. In this case, your real intention
was to say *no* and focus on what you *really wanted* to do (ie: write your paper).

STEP 1: SELF-AWARENESS

TIPS FOR IDENTIFYING YOUR GOALS (Cont'd)

Be honest with yourself

Are you harbouring any hidden agendas? For example, securing
a much sought after promotion may not be what you really
want, but is simply an opportunity to impress your
colleagues and friends. You might even be running
parent-tapes – voices of authority from the past that
prompt you to behave in certain ways. They may have
served you well as a child, but are not always helpful
or effective for you as an adult. (Like agreeing to
stand in for your associate because of your need for
external approval?)

Finding out who you are, where have come from and
why you are here is critical to pursuing a protean, or self-
managed, career. This information acts as a compass to help
you navigate and achieve your own internal psychological
success, that is, *your path with a heart*.

THE FIVE STEPS TO EMOTIONAL INTELLIGENCE

STEP 1: SELF-AWARENESS

SETTING YOUR GOALS

Steps to setting exceptional goals and finding *your path with a heart*:

1. State your goal in the positive (what you want rather than don't want)
2. Own it
3. Make it sensory specific (What will it feel like when you have achieved your goal? What will it sound like? What will it look like?)
4. Check the ecology (Is it something you really, really want? What or who else might be affected when you have achieved your goal?)
5. Identify the resources you need and go for it!

This can be remembered by using an NLP technique, which Julie Hay has developed into **POSIE**:

P ositive statement

O wned by the initiator (you)

S ensory-based

I ntention preserved (What will you gain or lose?)

E cology check (Remember, we exist in a system, family, friends, work: if you achieve your outcome, what or who else might be affected?)

THE FIVE STEPS TO EMOTIONAL INTELLIGENCE

STEP 2: EMOTION MANAGEMENT

> *There is nothing either good or bad but thinking makes it so*
> William Shakespeare, *Hamlet*

FIVE STEPS TO EMOTIONAL INTELLIGENCE

STEP 2: EMOTION MANAGEMENT

Managing your emotions effectively involves becoming mindful of those behaviours that really don't get you anywhere. You might feel great at winning a shouting match with a difficult colleague or customer, but this is a short-term gain and transitory. You may have lost a potential major client and done nothing to build effective relationships. In addition, raising your adrenalin levels, that is evoking the fight or flight response, will do nothing for your physical and psychological well-being!

By understanding the link between your interpretation of an event and your responses to it, you can choose an alternative way to feel. Being mindful is a key EI capability. Using the feeling diary will help you to identify the interaction between your thoughts, feelings and actions.

STEP 2: EMOTION MANAGEMENT

THE DYNAMICS OF EMOTION

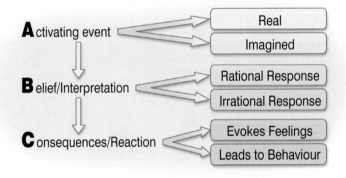

Activating event → Real

Imagined

Belief/Interpretation → Rational Response

Irrational Response

Consequences/Reaction → Evokes Feelings

Leads to Behaviour

THE FIVE STEPS TO EMOTIONAL INTELLIGENCE

STEP 2: EMOTION MANAGEMENT

As the Greek philosopher Epictetus said, *People are disturbed not only by things, but by the views they take of them*. What this means is that you can become **mindful** and then **choose** how you see and react in a situation. For example, look at the picture on the next page: do you see an older lady or a young lady? Ask a colleague to look at the picture: do they see what you see?

Remember, our beliefs, values, drivers and the rules we live by create our map of reality. If we can begin to recognise the way in which we delete, distort and discount important information, and make decisions on the basis of little real evidence (simply our own perceptions) we can begin to see how much of our emotional life is influenced by our map of the world. Change the map and you change how you see, hear, feel and behave in the world.

You can change your interpretation of what you see and you can change your responses to it. No one can make us *feel* anything.

THE FIVE STEPS TO EMOTIONAL INTELLIGENCE

STEP 2: EMOTION MANAGEMENT

*Leeper's
ambiguous lady*

THE FIVE STEPS TO EMOTIONAL INTELLIGENCE

STEP 2: EMOTION MANAGEMENT
WORRY BUSTER TECHNIQUE

When you find yourself becoming anxious or angry, or become worried about undertaking some task (eg: a presentation) adopt the *worry buster* technique. Ask yourself the following questions:

- Where is the evidence for the way I am thinking?
- What is the logic in my interpretation?
- What do I have to lose if I do/say this?
- What do I have to gain if I do/say this?
- What would be the worst that could happen if I do/don't say or do this?
- What can I learn from saying/doing this?

THE FIVE STEPS TO EMOTIONAL INTELLIGENCE

STEP 2: EMOTION MANAGEMENT
APPLYING THE WORRY BUSTER TECHNIQUE

1. Specify the situation/problem or worry (in specific terms – only facts)
2. Ask yourself: *what is the worst that can happen?*
3. Ask yourself: *will it kill me?*
4. Write a statement resolving to accept the worst should it occur
5. Consider what specific steps you will take to begin immediately to improve upon the worst possible outcome

Learn to live with worries:
- Live one day at a time
- Get the facts
- Practise the worry buster technique
- Adopt the six-second rule

The six-second rule is so called because six seconds is the time it takes to capture the *flight* or *fight* response (ie: avoid the emotional hijacking). When someone has said or done something that triggers your hot button, take a deep breath and count six seconds before you respond. Just try it – what is the worst that can happen?

THE FIVE STEPS TO EMOTIONAL INTELLIGENCE

STEP 2: EMOTION MANAGEMENT
THE 5-STEP FREEZE-FRAME TECHNIQUE

Another strategy for developing our capacity to manage our emotions is the 'freeze-frame' technique based on the HeartMath system, what Doc Childre describes as 'one-minute stress management':

1. Recognise stressful feelings and freeze-frame them. Take time out!

2. Make a concerted effort to shift your focus away from the racing mind or disturbing emotion(s).

3. Be calm and recall a positive, fun feeling that you have had and re-experience it.

4. Ask your heart, *What's a more effective response to this stressful situation?*

5. Listen and do what your heart says.

Source: EQ vs. IQ by Cynthia Kemper, *Communications World,* 1999

See also *Freeze Frame*, Doc Childre (www.planetarypub.com)

STEP 3: SELF-MOTIVATION

E-motion – is the spirit that moves

THE FIVE STEPS TO EMOTIONAL INTELLIGENCE

STEP 3: SELF-MOTIVATION

Motivation comes from the Latin *to move*.
As human beings we are goal-oriented, and
being self-motivated means pursuing our goals
with commitment, passion, energy and persistence.

In order to achieve high levels of motivation,
overcome setbacks and perform at our best,
we need to be able to manage our own
internal states, harness our emotions and
channel them in a direction that enables us
to achieve positive outcomes for our happiness
and well-being.

THE FIVE STEPS TO EMOTIONAL INTELLIGENCE

STEP 3: SELF-MOTIVATION

Being self-motivated calls for four essential actions.
You can remember them by using the acronym **SAME**:

1. Adopt positive **Self-talk**
2. Build an effective support network (your '**A**' team*)
3. Visualise an inspirational **Mentor** (real or fictitious)
4. Create a conducive **Environment** (air, light, sound, visual images)

*Research shows that people with effective 'A' teams enjoy better psychological health and are able to bounce back after setbacks.

THE FIVE STEPS TO EMOTIONAL INTELLIGENCE

STEP 3: SELF-MOTIVATION

ADOPT POSITIVE SELF-TALK

To develop an excellent inner-voice (positive self-talk) follow Janet's example:

Janet's goal is to feel better about herself, to increase her self-esteem. She, therefore, writes out the following:

I, Janet, am more and more pleasing to myself every day.
You, Janet, are more and more pleasing to yourself every day.
She, Janet, is more and more pleasing to herself every day.

I, Janet, am beginning to like myself as a woman.
You, Janet, are beginning to like yourself as a woman.
She, Janet, is beginning to like herself as a woman.

She writes out each affirmation three times, in the first, second and third persons. This is because our current views of ourselves are usually formed by a mixture of what we tell ourselves, what others tell us and what others say about us.

Affirmations are always written in the positive sense, so there are no negatives – not *I am not tense any more* **but** *I am relaxed*.

THE FIVE STEPS TO EMOTIONAL INTELLIGENCE

STEP 3: SELF-MOTIVATION

 ADOPT POSITIVE SELF-TALK

Here are some suggested statements with which you can practise positive self-talk. Write in your own name and repeat the exercise in the second and third person.

I,	am beautiful and loveable
I,	am talented, intelligent and creative
I,	am growing cleverer every day
I,	have much to offer, and others recognise this
I,	am getting slimmer every day
I,	am getting on better with … every day
I,	have a really beautiful nose
I,	have a lovely sense of humour that others appreciate very much
I,	am beginning to forgive … for …
I,	am getting over my disappointment at …
I,	am working on that report so that it will be finished by …
I,	am confident and can speak my mind clearly and confidently at meetings
I,	am becoming nicer every day
I,	am becoming happier every day

Alternatively you could read your affirmations into a tape and play it in your car, while in bed at night, or in the morning to wake you up – what a splendid way to start the day!

Source: adapted from *Managing Yourself,* Mike Pedler and Tom Boydell, 1999

THE FIVE STEPS TO EMOTIONAL INTELLIGENCE

STEP 3: SELF-MOTIVATION

 BUILD YOUR 'A' TEAM

To build an effective 'A' team, think about people who are in your current personal and organisational networks. Using the form below, write down the names of those colleagues, friends or associates who currently provide you with different kinds of support. If you have any gaps, you need to identify how these might be filled.

Types of support	At work	Away from work
Someone I can always rely on		
Someone I just enjoy chatting to		
Someone with whom I can discuss the exercises I am completing in this book		
Someone who makes me feel valued		
Someone who can give me honest feedback		
Someone who is always a valuable source of information		
Someone who will challenge me to sit up and take a good look at myself		
Someone I can depend on in a crisis		
Someone I feel close to		
Someone I can share bad news with		
Someone I can share good news and good feelings with		
Someone who introduces me to new ideas, new interests and new people		

THE FIVE STEPS TO EMOTIONAL INTELLIGENCE

STEP 3: SELF-MOTIVATION
VISUALISE AN INSPIRATIONAL MENTOR

Sports psychologists help successful athletes to use visualisation to enable them to create the right internal (mental) state in which to engage in their sport. Whether this is an image of winning a gold medal or breaking a *PB* (personal best) the aim is to achieve a state of *flow*. This is an internal state that energises and aligns emotions with the task in hand.

Two decades of research by the U.S. based psychologist Czikszentmihalyi show that activities that both challenge and permit us to draw on existing knowledge are most likely to send us into a state of *flow*. Daniel Goleman describes *flow* as the harnessing of our emotions to achieve superior performance and learning.

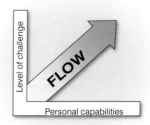

THE FIVE STEPS TO EMOTIONAL INTELLIGENCE

STEP 3: SELF-MOTIVATION

VISUALISE & ANCHOR AN INSPIRATIONAL MENTOR

To visualise an inspirational figure (mentor):

1. Think of someone (either real or imaginary) whom you consider to be inspirational (eg: Martin Luther King, Mother Theresa, Capt. Scarlett).

2. Create an image of that person in your mind's eye at their most inspiring (eg: Martin Luther King's *I have a dream* speech).

3. Imagine they are on a TV screen, turn up the colour and sound so that you are able to experience the feelings that the scene evokes.

4. When the feelings are at their peak, introduce a key word or a touch that you can use as an anchor, a trigger to evoke the image and associated feelings.

5. Repeat a number of times to ensure that you are able to fire off this *anchor* when you need to be inspired.

6. Test out your visualisation and ask the following question: *If* (name of mentor) *were here now, what would she/he/it say or do?*

STEP 3: SELF-MOTIVATION

VISUALISE AN INSPIRATIONAL MENTOR

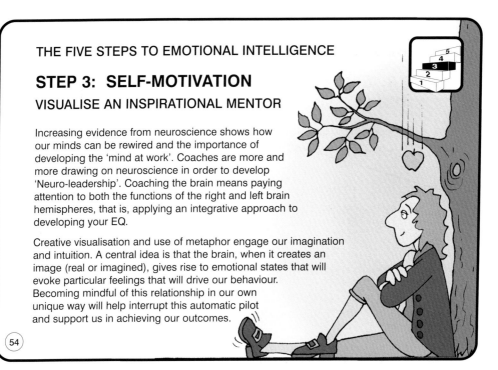

Increasing evidence from neuroscience shows how our minds can be rewired and the importance of developing the 'mind at work'. Coaches are more and more drawing on neuroscience in order to develop 'Neuro-leadership'. Coaching the brain means paying attention to both the functions of the right and left brain hemispheres, that is, applying an integrative approach to developing your EQ.

Creative visualisation and use of metaphor engage our imagination and intuition. A central idea is that the brain, when it creates an image (real or imagined), gives rise to emotional states that will evoke particular feelings that will drive our behaviour. Becoming mindful of this relationship in our own unique way will help interrupt this automatic pilot and support us in achieving our outcomes.

THE FIVE STEPS TO EMOTIONAL INTELLIGENCE

STEP 3: SELF-MOTIVATION

CREATE AN EI ENVIRONMENT

Think of a place where you were happiest. What did you see and hear? Was there plenty of light? Inspirational images? Identify what you need to have around you to make you feel motivated.

To create an environment that is conducive to developing high EI, make sure your environment meets the following criteria:

1. Healthy and helpful:
   - Is the air clean?
   - Can you hear helpful sounds?

2. Light:
   - Is it a motivator?

3. Contains motivators that you can surround yourself with, such as:
   - Pictures (Of your inspirational mentor, perhaps?)
   - People
   - Phrases

4. Organised:
   - Clear your desk, clear your mind

THE FIVE STEPS TO EMOTIONAL INTELLIGENCE

STEP 3: SELF-MOTIVATION

CREATE AN EI ENVIRONMENT

Research shows that music enhances performance. As the accelerated learning guru Dr Georgi Lazanov notes: *A well-executed concert can do about 60% of the presenting work in about 5% of the time.*

Well-chosen music can lead to:
- Lower levels of stress
- Improvements in long-term memory and retention
- Higher levels of creativity
- Enhanced learning
- Desired emotional states (relaxed, energised, focused, cleansed, creative, uplifted)

For more information read *Tune Your Brain* by Elizabeth Miles, Berkeley Books, 1997

THE FIVE STEPS TO EMOTIONAL INTELLIGENCE

INTERPERSONAL INTELLIGENCE (STEPS 4 & 5)

This next section focuses on what Goleman calls social intelligence, that is, steps four and five in the 5-step model. These final dimensions are concerned with *relationship management* and are key to our interpersonal (social) intelligence, the outer-intelligence we use to understand, navigate and then manage our interactions with others.

STEP 4: RELATIONSHIP MANAGEMENT

> *The ways that people treat us are reflections of the ways we treat ourselves.*
> Linda Field, *The Self-Esteem Workbook*

> *Neuroscience has discovered our brain's very design makes it sociable, inexorably drawn into an intimate brain-to-brain linkup whenever we engage with another person. That neural bridge lets us affect the brain – and so the body – of everyone we interact with, just as they do with us!*
> Daniel Goleman in *Social Intelligence*, 2006

THE FIVE STEPS TO EMOTIONAL INTELLIGENCE

STEP 4: RELATIONSHIP MANAGEMENT

Research shows that relationships are vital for personal growth and well-being. In the current climate of uncertainty, relationships have become strained and dysfunctional and major sources of stress at work.

The *psychological contract*, that is the implied expectations between an employee and employer, has undergone radical changes. The advent of the protean (self-managed) career is one which is driven by the individual. Employment relationships are now transactional and transitory. Research shows that individuals are likely to change their careers at least nine times and the removal of the compulsory retirement age in the UK could see this increase.

Pursuing an emotionally intelligent, self-managed career means that effective relationship management is critical to building social capital. That is, a protean career is dependent upon a constellation of relationships, a network that provides different sources of support.

THE FIVE STEPS TO EMOTIONAL INTELLIGENCE

STEP 4: RELATIONSHIP MANAGEMENT

Defining a relationship: *The coming together of two or more people for their mutual benefit.*

Types of relationship:
- Personal partnerships
- Friendships
- Relationships with work colleagues

Reasons why we get together:
- Companionship
- Sense of belonging
- Establish a support system
- Build our identity
- Personal development
- Love
- Enhance a sense of common purpose
- Develop a sense of teamwork
- Build our social capital

THE FIVE STEPS TO EMOTIONAL INTELLIGENCE

STEP 4: RELATIONSHIP MANAGEMENT

Reasons why relationships fail:

- Unrealistic expectations
- Lack of empathy
- Immaturity (low EI!)
- Dependency/co-dependency
- Inability to assert own needs
- Poor communication
- Ineffective strategies for conflict resolution
- Personality differences (different maps of the world)

THE FIVE STEPS TO EMOTIONAL INTELLIGENCE

STEP 4: RELATIONSHIP MANAGEMENT

What makes an effective relationship?

1. Reciprocity

This means meeting each other's needs: *You support – I support*. For example, if you repeatedly ask colleagues for help, advice or information, but do not find time to respond to their enquiries, eventually they will withhold their know-how and support. (Think of how that would impact on the organisation and your social capital.) Often it is only in repeated interactions that we can begin to identify the real needs of an individual. Check out your perceptions (remember Leeper's Ambiguous Lady?).

2. Skills

- *Dynamic listening:* Actively listen by paying attention to both verbal and non-verbal cues to identify what is really being said/or not said.

- *Establish empathy:* Step into their shoes and tune into their language to access their map of reality.

- *Use questions:* Directly ask what an individual's needs are. Don't mind-read.

THE FIVE STEPS TO EMOTIONAL INTELLIGENCE

STEP 4: RELATIONSHIP MANAGEMENT

3. Relating over time

- *Continuity:* Build up a picture of the other person. See them in different situations and different contexts in order to gather clues about who the person is, their beliefs, values and hot buttons. This will help you to relate better.

- *Build trust:* Establishing rapport involves trust and comfort, both of which need to be nurtured. Learn from each interaction and use this new knowledge to ensure subsequent interactions are positive and productive.

4. Engage in exchange

To build an effective relationship, exchange factual information, thoughts, feelings and ideas. It is an interactive process: what you disclose has an impact on the other person, which affects how you respond. **Remember, the ways people treat us are reflections of the ways we treat ourselves. Relationships are not made outside, they are made inside.**

THE FIVE STEPS TO EMOTIONAL INTELLIGENCE

STEP 4: RELATIONSHIP MANAGEMENT

Tips for sharing thoughts, feelings and ideas:

- Be in a good frame of mind
- Tune into how the other person responds
- Set a positive tone to the discussion
- Check out any feelings of discomfort

Remember, when we communicate our emotions:

55% is non-verbal (through our body language)
38% is the tone of voice
7% is dependent on the content (the actual words we use)

> *It ain't what you say, it's the way that you say it!*
> 1980s pop band Fun Boy Three

THE FIVE STEPS TO EMOTIONAL INTELLIGENCE

STEP 4: RELATIONSHIP MANAGEMENT

Six steps to building effective relationships:

1. Know the boundaries of the relationships (what can and can't be said or done; behaviours that are acceptable outside of work may be inappropriate within the workplace)

2. Check out expectations (respective needs and wants)

3. Review your perceptions (avoid making assumptions on basis of little evidence)

4. Review the other person's perceptions of you (take a risk, ask yourself what is the worst that can happen – use the *worry buster* to help)

5. Examine interactions (consider what worked well or not so well, and why this might be the case)

6. Determine the desired outcomes (set exceptional goals that have **power**)

THE FIVE STEPS TO EMOTIONAL INTELLIGENCE

STEP 4: RELATIONSHIP MANAGEMENT

Top ten tips for building exceptional relationships with colleagues at work:

1. Appreciate their individual skills, knowledge and capabilities
2. Make time to get to know them and actively listen to what they have to say
3. Remember, you can have a good relationship without having to be their bosom pals
4. If you have a disagreement with someone, look for an early solution
5. Spend some social time as well as work time with them
6. Give positive feedback for a job well done (as Manuel London of AT&T once said, *without feedback there is no learning*)
7. Seek their advice and opinions whenever you can
8. Support them through the tough times
9. Recognise individual uniqueness, be flexible in your style and approach, understand their *map of reality*
10. Use common courtesies and friendly greetings (research shows that leaders have a powerful impact on the emotional climate within a workgroup; being miserable can be contagious!)

THE FIVE STEPS TO EMOTIONAL INTELLIGENCE

STEP 4: RELATIONSHIP MANAGEMENT
FINAL THOUGHT

Most people who work have to work with other people. No matter how enjoyable a job is, it can become stressful and unfulfilling or downright miserable if human relationships break down. The first thing to realise and accept is that you cannot change other people. All you can do is to change yourself.

When someone says or does something to annoy you, *the annoyance is not in the thing being done, but in your response to the thing that is being done*. Things and actions are not in themselves annoying: the annoyance lies within ourselves, in the response.

> *If you keep on doing what you have always done, you will keep on getting what you have always got!*

THE FIVE STEPS TO EMOTIONAL INTELLIGENCE

STEP 5: EMOTION COACHING

Managers need to change their whole approach to managing and instead of relying on systems and control procedures, need to get to know and trust their people as individuals … Direct personal contact and coaching keeps managers appraised of real business challenges and provides an opportunity to shape responses through a shared understanding. The new corporation is the individualised corporation.

S. Goshal & C. Bartlett, *Harvard Business Review*, May-June 1995

Leadership coaching has become a key to success for both individuals and organisations.
David Gergen, Centre for Public Leadership, Harvard

THE FIVE STEPS TO EMOTIONAL INTELLIGENCE

STEP 5: EMOTION COACHING

A significant shift since the first edition of this book has been the rapid and explosive growth in coaching, not only in terms of its development as a profession, but in developing managers' capacity to coach. It is big business, and even in the recession the 2011 CIPD Learning & Talent Development Report (L&TD) notes this is one area in which organisations are continuing to invest. The fifth and final step of the model looks at ways in which to develop as an emotion coach (E-Coach).

Being an 'E-Coach' means helping others to:

- Develop their EQ capabilities
- Resolve conflict
- Be solution-focused
- Communicate effectively
- Become motivated

THE FIVE STEPS TO EMOTIONAL INTELLIGENCE

STEP 5: EMOTION COACHING
E-COACH CAPABILITIES

To become an exceptional EQ coach you need to *know:*

- What coaching means (as distinct from other learning roles)
- What the coaching process entails and what relevant models to use
- How to manage the relationship and agree the boundaries
- Where coaching fits within the overall scheme of things, ie what it is designed to achieve. (Is it to drive organisational change as an integral feature of a leadership/OD intervention? Or raise performance? Or maximise potential?)
- How people respond to change and how to overcome resistance to change
- How people learn and how to assess differences in learning styles
- How to apply different psychological models and ways of assessing values, beliefs, motivation, personality (and emotional intelligence)
- What competencies need to be developed, either personally or for a specific job role

THE FIVE STEPS TO EMOTIONAL INTELLIGENCE

STEP 5: EMOTION COACHING
E-COACH CAPABILITIES

What *skills* do you need to become an exceptional EQ coach? You need to:

- Actively listen (to what is being said and not said – use your intuition)
- Use different questioning techniques to get beneath the surface and challenge the underlying problem, not the surface issue
- Influence, persuade and challenge (knowing when to adopt different styles)
- Engage in solution-focused approaches, using creativity techniques and appreciative inquiry to look at problems in a different way
- Have good time/personal management skills
- Help the learner to set goals and identify possible strategies
- Network and access resources that will help the learner
- Help the learner to put together an Action Plan, to identify enablers and disablers towards achieving their goals

THE FIVE STEPS TO EMOTIONAL INTELLIGENCE

STEP 5: EMOTION COACHING
E-COACH CAPABILITIES

What *behaviours* do you need to demonstrate? You need to:

- Demonstrate empathy and capacity to build rapport
- Act as an EI role model
- Be non-judgemental
- Maintain confidentiality
- Signpost learner to other sources of support (recognising your own limitations and gaps in learning)
- Continually engage in a critical evaluation of your own performance and take action
- Be committed to your own personal and on-going development
- Continually seek to build learner's confidence and self-esteem, to open their horizons

THE FIVE STEPS TO EMOTIONAL INTELLIGENCE

STEP 5: EMOTION COACHING

E-COACH CAPABILITIES

What *qualities* and *experiences* should you possess? You should have:

- Experience of supporting learners
- Experience of being coached or mentored
- A sense of humour
- Tact and diplomacy
- Ability to demonstrate integrity
- Capacity to show evidence of persistence and resilience
- A willingness to share own learning experiences (successes and failures)
- Confidence in your own abilities
- Passion when embracing your role as E-coach
- Capability to be congruent, journeying along your *path with a heart*
- Emotional intelligence!

STEP 5: EMOTION COACHING
ROLE OF THE E-COACH

The explosion in coaching, with an increasing number of professional bodies and consultancies offering their own brand or model of coaching, makes it a challenge to navigate this burgeoning market. See the section on further reading for useful resources. While different schools train coaches in an array of approaches, at the simplest level a coaching conversation includes the following four elements:

1. An assessment of where the coachee is now.
2. Identification of outcomes (goals) of where they want to go.
3. Planning how to get there (identifying strategies).
4. Gathering feedback on results.

One approach I use with clients is an 8-step process: Diagnosis; Alliance; Assessment; Analysis; Alternatives; Action Planning; Application; Review and Evaluation. We'll look at this in more detail on the following pages.

STEP 5: EMOTION COACHING

ROLE OF THE E-COACH

1. Diagnosis

I meet the person and their sponsor on a 1:1 basis to begin the contracting process, ie to:

- Establish benchmarks (outcomes) for the coaching: what is going to be observed as a result of this intervention? Typically my assignments might involve: behavioural coaching (for EQ); conflict coaching (as part of a transformational mediation); crisis coaching (individuals experiencing forced change) and transition coaching (coaching for meaning and purpose)

- Encourage self-reflection to engage the potential coachee in the process. I get them to rate themselves against a set of personal and professional competencies, as to where they are now and their aspirations (and sponsor expectations)

- Agree the contract and mechanisms for giving feedback

An essential feature of this step is to establish whether there is chemistry between myself and the potential client. Without this relational element of contracting, the process is a non-starter. As part of contracting with the sponsor, I take the line that only broad themes will be reported back and related to the specific outcomes of the coaching assignment. Establishing the boundaries of the relationship, eg confidentiality, ensures the foundation of trust.

THE FIVE STEPS TO EMOTIONAL INTELLIGENCE

STEP 5: EMOTION COACHING

ROLE OF THE E-COACH

2. Alliance

This is the first meeting during which:

- The purpose of the coaching is outlined
- A clear set of outcomes are agreed (remember **POSIE**, see page 37)
- Specific assessment tools are identified

3. Assessment

Here an audit is undertaken of existing and desired competencies, strengths and weaknesses. As the E-coach, I:

- Use plenty of open questions
- Reflect and summarise to help the learner explore themselves and begin to develop their self-awareness
- Use particular psychometric tools and other exercises which might include: career and interest inventories; personal and working styles; personality questionnaires; and, if the assignment is specifically designed to develop EI capabilities, specific EQ measures such as the Boston EI-Q (version 2) both self-report and 360-degree feedback

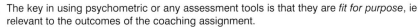

The key in using psychometric or any assessment tools is that they are *fit for purpose*, ie relevant to the outcomes of the coaching assignment.

THE FIVE STEPS TO EMOTIONAL INTELLIGENCE

STEP 5: EMOTION COACHING
ROLE OF THE E-COACH

4. Analysis
During this session the learner and I:
- Use assessment information to identify existing capabilities and prioritise development areas, using such frameworks as SWOT (Strengths/Weaknesses/Opportunities/Threats)
- Discuss appropriate models or competency frameworks (eg: *5-steps to EI*)
- Prioritise development actions

5. Alternatives
Here we:
- Consider alternative ways in which to work on development areas
- Use problem-solving strategies to explore options and possibilities (enablers and disablers)
- Use a structured process for decision-making – checking out what is realistic and practical

THE FIVE STEPS TO EMOTIONAL INTELLIGENCE

STEP 5: EMOTION COACHING
ROLE OF THE E-COACH

6. Action Planning
Here we:
- Devise a detailed plan
- Identify sources of support/hindrance
- Agree timescales

It is important as an E-Coach to use an appropriate mix of challenge and support, that is to move along this continuum in order to facilitate the achievement of outcomes.

7. Application
Here the learner undertakes the actions agreed, which may include:
- Behavioural exercises (doing something different, like communicating with a colleague in a different way, chairing a meeting, physically walking-the-job)
- Reading articles/books on issues that are relevant to the development plan
- Exercises such as life/career essay; personal and career evaluations
- Practising mindfulness
- Keeping a feeling diary

THE FIVE STEPS TO EMOTIONAL INTELLIGENCE

STEP 5: EMOTION COACHING
ROLE OF THE E-COACH

8. Review, Feedback and Evaluation
Here the learner:
- Discusses thoughts, feelings and outcomes of actions undertaken
- Identifies what worked well and not so well
- Explores key learning points
- Agrees further development actions with the coach

At the end of the programme, evaluation of outcomes is carried out between coach and learner, coach and sponsor, and learner and sponsor.

(A useful article on *How to Evaluate Coaching* was published in *Coaching at Work*, Vol.4, Issue 2, contact mc@eicoaching.co.uk for a copy or go to: www.coaching-at-work.com)

THE FIVE STEPS TO EMOTIONAL INTELLIGENCE

STEP 5: EMOTION COACHING
ROLE OF THE E-COACH

You can use this 8-step framework for the coaching programme and for individual sessions, thus meeting essential key elements of:

1. An assessment of where the learner is now
2. Identification of where the learner wants to get to
3. Planning how to get there
4. Feedback on results

ASSESSING & DEVELOPING YOUR EMOTIONAL INTELLIGENCE

ASSESSING YOUR EMOTIONAL INTELLIGENCE

Having introduced the 5-step model for developing EI, now is a useful point at which to establish just where you are on an EI scale. Complete the Boston EI-Q (short version) to assess your current level of EI and identify those capabilities that you need to work on. Use the EI development plan (on page 89) to help you focus your energies. Find a coach; take action; use the exercises in this book and then afterwards re-assess your EI.

The Boston Emotional Intelligence Questionnaire (Boston EI-Q) is copyright of Chapman & Clarke at EI Coaching and arises out of substantial research as reported in Clarke, R. Goldsmiths College, University of London (2000), a study exploring the link between emotional intelligence and stress in front-line police officers.

Enjoy the journey!

ASSESSING & DEVELOPING YOUR EMOTIONAL INTELLIGENCE

THE BOSTON EI QUESTIONNAIRE

The following questions are designed to help you establish just how aware you are of your emotional responses and how well you use your emotional intelligence.

The questionnaire follows the 5-step model of EI. For each question tick the box that comes closest to how you feel about the answer.

	A	B	C	D
1. Can you tell when your mood is changing?	Always	Sometimes	Rarely	Never
2. Do you know when you are becoming defensive?	Always	Sometimes	Rarely	Never
3. Can you tell when your emotions are affecting your performance?	Always	Sometimes	Rarely	Never
4. How quickly do you realise you are starting to lose your temper?	Very quickly	Not very quickly	Slowly	Very slowly
5. How soon do you realise that your thoughts are turning negative?	Straightaway	Quite soon	After a while	Usually too late

© Chapman & Clarke (2001)

(83)

THE BOSTON EI QUESTIONNAIRE

	A	B	C	D
6. Can you relax when you are under pressure?	Very easily	Quite easily	Hardly ever	Not at all
7. Do you *just get on with things* when you are angry?	Usually	Sometimes	Not usually	Never
8. Do you engage in *self-talk* to vent feelings of anger or anxiety?	Often	Sometimes	Rarely	Never
9. Do you remain cool in the face of others' anger or aggression?	Always	Usually	Occasionally	Never
10. How well can you concentrate when you are feeling anxious?	Very well	Quite well	Just about	Not at all

THE BOSTON EI QUESTIONNAIRE

	A	B	C	D
11. Do you *bounce back* quickly after a setback?	Always	Sometimes	Occasionally	Never
12. Do you deliver on your promises?	Without fail	Quite often	Rarely	Never
13. Can you *kick start* yourself into action when appropriate?	Yes, always	Yes, sometimes	Not often	No, never
14. How willingly do you change the way you do things when current methods are not working?	Very willingly	Quite willingly	Quite reluctantly	Very reluctantly
15. Are you able to lift your energy level to tackle and complete *boring tasks*?	Always	Usually	Rarely	Never

ASSESSING & DEVELOPING YOUR EMOTIONAL INTELLIGENCE

THE BOSTON EI QUESTIONNAIRE

	A	**B**	**C**	**D**
16. Do you actively seek ways of resolving conflict?	Yes, often	Yes, sometimes	Not often	Never
17. To what extent do you influence others about the way things are done?	A great extent	To some extent	Very little	None
18. How willing are you to act as a spokesperson for others?	Very willing	Can be persuaded	Quite reluctantly	Not at all willing
19. Are you able to demonstrate empathy with others' feelings?	Always	Sometimes	Rarely	Never
20. To what extent do you find that others trust and confide in you?	Frequently	Occasionally	Hardly ever	Never

THE BOSTON EI QUESTIONNAIRE

	A	B	C	D
21. Do you find yourself able to raise morale and make others feel good?	Yes, often	Yes, sometimes	Rarely	Never
22. How freely do you offer help and assistance to others?	Very freely	Quite freely	Reluctantly	Not freely at all
23. Can you sense when others are feeling angry or anxious and respond appropriately?	Yes, always	Yes, often	Hardly ever	Never
24. How effective are you at communicating your feelings to others?	Very	Quite	Not very	Not at all
25. Do you contribute to the management of conflict and emotion within your work group or family?	Yes, often	Yes, sometimes	Rarely	Never

THE BOSTON EI QUESTIONNAIRE

MARKING YOUR ANSWERS

Give yourself 4 points for each box ticked in column A, 3 points for each box ticked in column B, 2 for C and 1 for D. Enter the scores in the boxes below and fill in the totals.

Question

1	2	3	4	5	**Total** (Questions 1-5)
☐	☐	☐	☐	☐	☐ Your score for **Self-awareness**
6	7	8	9	10	**Total** (Questions 6-10)
☐	☐	☐	☐	☐	☐ Your score for **Emotion management**
11	12	13	14	15	**Total** (Questions 11-15)
☐	☐	☐	☐	☐	☐ Your score for **Self-motivation**
16	17	18	19	20	**Total** (Questions 16-20)
☐	☐	☐	☐	☐	☐ Your score for **Relationship management**
21	22	23	24	25	**Total** (Questions 21-25)
☐	☐	☐	☐	☐	☐ Your score for **Emotion coaching**

If you scored 17 or more on any dimension you seem to shape up pretty well. A score of 13 to 16 indicates some remedial work is necessary. 12 to 9 *roll up your sleeves*. 8 or less means *oh dear*! But do not despair whatever your score. Now that you understand emotional intelligence you will be able to develop your own EI.

ASSESSING & DEVELOPING YOUR EMOTIONAL INTELLIGENCE

EI DEVELOPMENT PLAN

5 steps to emotional intelligence	My EI development goal(s) are (using POSIE)	How am I going to achieve my goal(s)? Development actions	What do I need to help me? Support/ resources	When am I going to achieve my goal(s) Time-scales
1. Self-awareness				
2. Emotion management				
3. Self-motivation				
4. Relationship management				
5. Emotion coaching				

ASSESSING & DEVELOPING YOUR EMOTIONAL INTELLIGENCE

WHAT CAN I DO TO RAISE MY EI?

- The first step is to identify your own emotions. (Use the feeling word list opposite to help you.)

- Take responsibility for them. (This is much harder.)

- Learn what compassion and empathy are. (This is much easier if you have taken the first two steps; impossible if you haven't!)

- Read books on emotions. (Consult the *mind, body & soul* section of any good book shop.)

- Get involved with learning, Continuous Professional Development or other networks.

- Find a quiet place/time to express your feelings. Keep a feeling journal.

- Read emotional literature, watch emotional movies, label the feelings being acted out. (Soaps are a good source for the full continuum of human emotions!)

- Develop mindfulness (visit www.bemindful.co.uk as a first step)

SOME *FEELING WORDS*

Respected
Optimistic
Supported
Discriminated against
Controlled
Needy
Disrespected
Unsupported
Obligated
In control
Free
Unmotivated
Appreciated
Mocked
Left out
Judged
Unappreciated
Encouraged
Undeserving
Accepted
Invalidated
Abandoned
Lectured to
Uncomfortable
Burdened
Sad
Hopeless
Rejected
Confident
Rewarded
Preached at
Criticised
Afraid
Lonely
Validated
Worthy
Unworthy
Motivated
Discouraged
Ignored
Out of control
Excited
Pessimistic
Incompetent
Important
Proud
Depressed
Unimportant
Fulfilled
Deserving
Jealous
Competent

TEN HABITS OF EMOTIONALLY INTELLIGENT PEOPLE

People with high EI:

1. Label their feelings, rather than labelling people or situations
2. Distinguish between thoughts and feelings
3. Take responsibility for their feelings
4. Use their emotions to help make decisions
5. Show respect for others' feelings
6. Feel energised, not angry
7. Validate others' feelings
8. Practise getting a positive value from their negative emotions
9. Don't advise, command, control, criticise, blame or judge others
10. Practise mindfulness

DEVELOPING AN EMOTIONALLY INTELLIGENT ORGANISATION

DEVELOPING AN EMOTIONALLY INTELLIGENT ORGANISATION

Top down, corporate-wide organisation development is becoming less consistent with contemporary organisational forms. The requirement on managers to deal effectively with more complex organisations places a greater premium on individual contribution, which in turn relies on meta-abilities…individual development is the starting point for organisation development.

Cranfield University, 1997

Leadership is about emotion.

Hooper & Potter, The Business of Leadership, 1997

DEVELOPING AN EMOTIONALLY INTELLIGENT ORGANISATION

EI AS A CHANGE MANAGEMENT STRATEGY

A key theme in this new edition is that organisational life, and with it leadership, has changed. Developing the EQ of leaders is a given in developing an EQ organisation. In this final section of the book I turn to look at ways in which EQ can be used as a change management strategy. The primary source is that offered by two writers, leaders in the field of emotional intelligence, Cary Cherniss and Mitchel Adler, who offer a four step process:

1. **S**ecure commitment
2. **P**repare for change
3. **T**rain and develop
4. **M**aintain and evaluate

A useful diagram follows on the next page, and on the following pages I describe how to use this framework in more detail.

EI AS A CHANGE MANAGEMENT STRATEGY

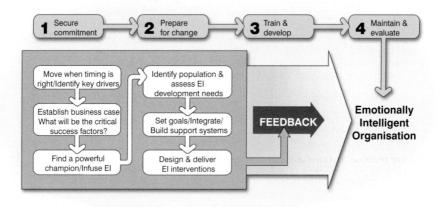

DEVELOPING AN EMOTIONALLY INTELLIGENT ORGANISATION

STEP 1: SECURE COMMITMENT

Get *buy-in* by answering the following questions:
- What are the key drivers or triggers for change, what *pain* exists within the business?
- How can EI help?
- What are the hot buttons for top management?
- Who are the key stakeholders and what's in it for them (WIFT)?
- What are the added value or bottom-line benefits for developing EI capabilities?
- How will you establish the critical success factors?
- Who has high EI and can champion the programme?
- Who is going to design the programme?
- How will EI be communicated or infused within the organisation?

Possible reasons for developing EI include:
- Increase performance and productivity
- Improve leadership capabilities
- Talent management
- Empowerment and engagement
- Enhance teams
- Build resilience
- Address outcomes from organisational DNA (Development Needs Assessment)

DEVELOPING AN EMOTIONALLY INTELLIGENT ORGANISATION

STEP 2: PREPARE FOR CHANGE

Having established the business case you now need to:
- Identify what EI capabilities need to be developed and are critical for successful performance
- Conduct a gap analysis between any existing competency frameworks and EI capabilities
- Assess EI development needs
- Identify possible participants
- Gauge readiness of the learners

Remember: EQ development is personal development and needs buy-in and personal commitment. Both my own and other coaching psychological research shows that the best EI intervention is one that involves the conjoint use of coaching (see Chapman, 2005; Grant et al. 2007).

You also need to establish:
- How the facilitators will convince learners that EI capabilities can be developed
- How the facilitators will demonstrate the WIFM factor to get individual buy-in
- The nature of and commitment to on-going support

DEVELOPING AN EMOTIONALLY INTELLIGENT ORGANISATION

STEP 2: PREPARE FOR CHANGE
CONDUCTING A COMPETENCY GAP ANALYSIS (CGA)

1. Do your homework, read around EI and understand what emotional capabilities mean and how they can make a difference (see *further reading* at end of book)
2. Review your existing competency frameworks and examine how EI capabilities *map* onto your existing models; you may like to use the following:

Our Competency	Self-awareness (knowing one's own internal states, preferences, resources & intuitions)	Our Competency	Self-management (managing one's own internal states, impulses & resources)
	Emotional awareness: recognising one's emotions & their effects		Self-control: keeping disruptive emotions & impulses in check
	Accurate self-assessment: knowing your strengths/limitations		Achievement drive: striving to improve or meet a standard of excellence; persistence in pursuing goals despite obstacles
	Self-confidence: a strong sense of self-worth		Conscientiousness & reliability: taking responsibility for personal performance; maintaining standards of honesty & integrity
			Adaptability: flexibility in handling change initiative & innovation
			Readiness to act on opportunities; being comfortable with novel ideas, approaches & information

Mapping existing competencies against EI dimensions

3. Identify those meta-EI capabilities that will differentiate star performers
4. Gain commitment and *buy-in* from all stakeholders
5. Communicate   **6.** Develop   **7.** Evaluate

DEVELOPING AN EMOTIONALLY INTELLIGENT ORGANISATION

STEP 3: TRAIN & DEVELOP

In designing and delivering the EI intervention you need to ask yourself:

- Who is best placed to facilitate?
- What resources are available?
- Do the facilitators display the necessary emotional competencies?
- How will I ensure that they do?
- What will be included in the design and how much time will be spent on cognitive vs experiential activities?
- How will real-time feedback be incorporated and handled?
- How will EI capabilities be practised back *on the job*?

As I noted earlier, *Without feedback there is no learning*. So, who is going to provide the support, what form of support will this be and how will you ensure this will happen?

EI

STEP 3: TRAIN & DEVELOP

ELEMENTS OF AN EFFECTIVE EI DEVELOPMENT PROGRAMME

Developing emotional capabilities means unlearning old habits of thought, feeling and action. It also involves commitment, motivation, sustained effort and practice. Kate Cannon was one of the first to develop an EI intervention in American Express. She advocates three simple principles, which continue to resonate a decade later:

1. **Theory**
   Background to EI and why it is important to develop it within the organisation

2. **Practice**
   Introduce core EI skills and allow learners to practise, practise, practise

3. **Application**
   Support for learners to apply the tools back on-the-job

(For a special report on ten years of EI, including case studies, look at *Coaching at Work*, Vol.4 Issue 4 (2009)).

DEVELOPING AN EMOTIONALLY INTELLIGENT ORGANISATION

STEP 3: TRAIN & DEVELOP

ELEMENTS OF AN EFFECTIVE EI DEVELOPMENT PROGRAMME

Tips for design:

- Use multi-sensory methods and media (music, pictures, stories, poetry) that tap into multiple intelligences
- Appeal to different learning styles and preferences
- Stage the training over a number of weeks
- Use small groups (established teams work best)
- Ensure learners practise during and between sessions and after formal training is complete
- Incorporate *real-time* and on-going feedback
- Allow for some *down-time* for learners to reflect on their own responses and those of others
- Incorporate assignments that can be integrated back on-the-job
- Use tips and techniques suggested in this book!

DEVELOPING AN EMOTIONALLY INTELLIGENT ORGANISATION

STEP 4: MAINTAIN & EVALUATE

Following the intervention, you need to make sure that:

1. There is on-going coaching and support
2. Coaches are trained
3. Other people management and development strategies encourage the improvement of EI capabilities
4. Line managers are involved and *buy-in* to the process is gained
5. EI capabilities are not just an add-on but are regarded as the core capabilities for successful performance
6. EI intervention is evaluated against established benchmarks (the critical success factors)

DEVELOPING AN EMOTIONALLY INTELLIGENT ORGANISATION

STEP 4: MAINTAIN & EVALUATE

EVALUATING EI INTERVENTIONS

In an article with Alison Carter in *Coaching at Work* (Vol.4, Issue 2, 2009) we outlined a 5-step approach to evaluation.

Step 1: Decide what to evaluate: Kirkpatrick's level of evaluation is useful here. That is, immediate reaction; transfer of learning that has taken place; observed behavioural change; impact on business performance/organisational matrices

Step 2: Measure changes over time: The most convincing evidence of ROI is that gathered longitudinally – at different points over time (pre and post); use a control group

Step 3: Do a Stakeholder Analysis: Identify the key stakeholders, then gather feedback against their expected outcomes

Step 4: Identify what will count as evidence: This depends on your analysis at Step 3. Generally, numbers serve to convince sponsors, while stories can be easily remembered

Step 5: Ensure evaluator competence: Be curious – go beyond Kirkpatrick!

DEVELOPING AN EMOTIONALLY INTELLIGENT ORGANISATION

EXAMPLE EI DEVELOPMENT PROGRAMME

Group size	16
Group characteristics	Established team
Structure	1 day a month for 5 months
Topics	• EI, what is it? • EI capabilities in relation to existing management competencies • Building a vision, eliciting values and setting powerful goals • Building effective relationships • Correcting faulty thinking (reframing using ABC) • Monitoring self in action • Identifying past patterns (negative self-talk & outdated tapes)

Media & methods	• Cognitive & experiential learning • Role plays, feedback • Peer E-coaching • Action learning • Music • Metaphors • ABC/Freeze-frame • Pairs/Self-disclosure • Personal action planning • Behavioural assignments
Support	• Managers trained as E-coaches
Evaluation	• Happy sheets • Pre- and post- 360° EI questionnaires (Boston EIQ) • Performance appraisals • Illuminative evaluation 1 year after initial programme

FINAL THOUGHTS & REFLECTIONS

EQ is...the ability to use emotions to help ... solve problems and live a more effective life. Emotional intelligence without intelligence, or intelligence without emotional intelligence, is only part of the solution. The complete solution is the head working with the heart.

David Caruso, Co-Author with Salovey & Mayer, of the MSCEIT

FURTHER READING

On Emotional Intelligence

David Caruso & Peter Salovey,
The Emotionally Intelligent Manager,
Jossey-Bass (2004)

Professional Journals:
*Competency & Emotional Intelligence Quarterly:
The Journal of Performance Through People*
(www.irseclipse.co.uk)

Cary Cherniss & Mitchel Adler,
Promoting Emotional Intelligence in Organizations,
American Society of Training & Development (2000)
(access via amazon.com)

Daniel Goleman, *Social Intelligence*,
Hutchinson (2006)

Daniel Goleman,
Working with Emotional Intelligence,
Bloomsbury (1998)

Daniel Goleman, Richard Boyatzis
& Annie McKee,
The New Leaders, Little, Brown (2002)

Dr. Hendrie Weisinger,
Emotional Intelligence at Work,
Jossey-Bass (1998)

Doc Childre & Howard Martin,
*The Heartmath Solution: Proven techniques
for Developing Emotional Intelligence*,
Piatkus, 1999

Richard Boyatzis & Annie McKee,
Resonant Leadership, HBR (2005)
(particularly chapter six on mindfulness)

FURTHER READING

Coaching, Coaching Psychology & Mentoring

Gillian Burn,
The NLP Pocketbook,
Management Pocketbooks (2005)

Ian Fleming & Allan J.D. Taylor,
The Coaching Pocketbook,
Management Pocketbooks (2003)

Jane Grant & Anthony M Grant,
Solution-Focused Coaching: Managing People in a Complex World, Pearson Education Ltd (2003)

Averil Leimon & Gladeana McMahon,
Positive Psychology for Dummies,
Wiley (2009)

Suzanne Skiffington & Perry Zeus,
Behavioral Coaching,
McGraw-Hill (2003)

John Whitmore,
Coaching for Performance,
Nicholas Brealey (2002)

Mindfulness

Jon Kabat-Zinn,
Wherever You Go, There You Are,
Piatkus (1994)

Mark Williams and Danny Penman,
Mindfulness: A Practical Guide to Finding Peace in a Frantic World, Piatkus (2011)

Michael Chaskalson, *The Mindful Workplace: Developing Resilient Individuals and Resonant Organizations with MBSR*,
Wiley-Blackwell (2011)

Useful Websites

www.associationforcoaching.com
www.bangor.ac.uk/mindfulness
www.bemindful.co.uk
www.coaching-at-work.com
www.eiconsortium.org
http://oxfordmindfulness.org

EI RESOURCES

EQ ASSESSMENT TOOLS

Since this book first appeared in 2001, writing in 2011 I can report that there has been an explosion in the number of assessment tools designed to measure EQ. These are often based on the authors' own model of emotional intelligence, or original personality questionnaires that have been revised to measure emotions. What this means in practical terms is that you need to decide the model that is the best fit for your purposes. I did some further research in 2007 that looked at strategies for developing executive EQ and the findings revealed that it didn't matter which measure you use, providing that it is consistent with the design of the development intervention. One caveat that is important in a burgeoning market is to make sure that the coaches/assessors possess relevant psychometric qualifications and specific training in the tool that they are using for EQ development.

Tools that have been established on the basis of primary research for over a decade are:

- Bar-On Emotional Quotient Inventory (www.mhs.com)
- Emotional Competence Inventory (based on the work of Goleman, www.ei.haygroup.com)
- Boston Emotional Intelligence Questionnaire (Boston EI-Q) (www.eicoaching.co.uk)
- Individual and Team Effectiveness Questionnaire (www.jca.biz)

EQ DEVELOPMENT

Over the last ten years I have been pleased at the number of people who have used this book across the world to support their EI interventions. Enter emotional intelligence into Google today and you will be overwhelmed at the range of services and individuals offering to develop your EQ. These are now too numerous to list. Instead of listing EI resources, here in this 2nd edition I am going to highlight trends that will impact on the design of EQ interventions:

- **Neuroscience** Goleman has already brought social intelligence to the market, which he asserts is a companion to emotional intelligence. Look at emerging work into Neuro-Leadership (www.NeuroLeadership.org)

- **Mindfulness** Extensive evidence shows the benefits and impact of mindfulness-based interventions on physical and psychological wellbeing – read anything by Jon Kabat-Zinn. A useful starting place is where the mindfulness-based stress reduction programme (MBSR) began, that is (http://www.umassmed.edu/cfm/home/index.aspx.). It is in the process of crossing over into the workplace

- **Resilience** is an outcome of EQ development, coaching and mindfulness practice. This is currently a priority area for organisations, along with talent management and engagement

About the Author

Margaret Chapman, BSc (Hons), AdvDipEdn, MSc, MEd, C.Psychol, AFBPsS, Registered Practitioner Psychologist (Occupational), Health Professions Council, Accredited Mediator

Margaret was one of the first occupational psychologists in the U.K. to research, develop and write about coaching psychology and emotional intelligence. She has presented her work nationally and internationally and has continuously asked the question 'How do you develop EQ?' Her own EQ journey has seen her fuse together training in NLP, Gestalt, Motivational Interviewing, Cognitive-Behavioural Therapy, Coaching for Happiness, Solution-Focused and existential approaches to develop an approach which she describes as *Integrative-Behavioural Coaching*. Since 2008 she has been developing her mindfulness practice and in 2011 talked publicly for the first time about mindfulness, mindful leadership and its relationship with developing emotional intelligence.

Ever passionate in sharing her experiences in the service of 'developing the developers' Margaret is currently writing a series of articles on this topic and plans to offer workshops and CPD for coaches looking to design their own mindfulness mosaic. Margaret is happy to provide copies of articles and or references/advice on research into EQ and potential access to the long version of the Boston EI-Q for research purposes. She can be reached at mc@eicoaching.co.uk

ORDER FORM

Your details

Name _____

Position _____

Company _____

Address _____

_____

_____

Telephone _____

Fax _____

E-mail _____

VAT No. (EC companies) _____

Your Order Ref _____

Please send me:

	No. copies
The Emotional Intelligence Pocketbook	☐
The _____ Pocketbook	☐
The _____ Pocketbook	☐
The _____ Pocketbook	☐

Order by Post
MANAGEMENT POCKETBOOKS LTD

LAUREL HOUSE, STATION APPROACH,
ALRESFORD, HAMPSHIRE SO24 9JH UK

Order by Phone, Fax or Internet
Telephone: +44 (0)1962 735573
Facsimile: +44 (0)1962 733637
Email: sales@pocketbook.co.uk
Web: www.pocketbook.co.uk

Customers in USA should contact:
Management Pocketbooks
2427 Bond Street, University Park, IL 60466
Telephone: 866 620 6944 Facsimile: 708 534 7803
Email: mp.orders@ware-pak.com
Web: www.managementpocketbooks.com